The Young King
and Other Stories

Oscar Wilde

Level 3

Retold by Sue Harmes

Series Editors: Andy Hopkins and Jocelyn Potter

Pearson Education Limited

Edinburgh Gate, Harlow,
Essex CM20 2JE, England
and Associated Companies throughout the world.

ISBN: 978-1-4479-6764-4

First edition published 2000
This edition published 2009

3 5 7 9 10 8 6 4

Text copyright © Penguin Books Ltd 2000
This edition copyright © Pearson Education Ltd 2009
Illustrations by Fátima García

Set in 11/13pt A. Garamond
Printed in China
SWTC/03
Produced for the Publishers by AC Estudio Editorial S.L.

Published by Pearson Education Ltd

Acknowledgements

We are grateful to the following for permission to reproduce photographs:

Jupiter Unlimited: Comstock Images 67; UNICEF / Thierry Delvigne-Jean: 66

*Every effort has been made to trace the copyright holders and we apologise in advance for any unintentional omissions.
We would be pleased to insert the appropriate acknowledgement in any subsequent edition of this publication.*

For a complete list of the titles available in the Pearson English Active Readers series, visit www.pearsonenglishactivereaders.com.
Alternatively, write to your local Pearson Education office or to
Pearson English Readers Marketing Department, Pearson Education, Edinburgh Gate, Harlow, Essex CM20 2JE, England.

Contents

	Activities 1	iv
Story 1	The Young King	1
Story 2	The Birthday of the Infanta	8
	Activities 2	14
Story 3	The Happy Prince	16
	Activities 3	24
Story 4	The Fisherman and his Soul	26
	Activities 4	38
Story 5	The Nightingale and the Rose	40
	Activities 5	46
Story 6	The Star Child	48
	Activities 6	58
Story 7	The Selfish Giant	60
	Talk about it	64
	Write about it	65
	Project: Helping Other People	66

1.1 What's the book about?

Match the pictures and the story titles. What do you think?

1 ☐ 'The Young King'
2 ☐ 'The Birthday of the Infanta'
3 ☐ 'The Happy Prince'
4 ☐ 'The Fisherman and his Soul'

5 ☐ 'The Nightingale and the Rose'
6 ☐ 'The Star Child'
7 ☐ 'The Selfish Giant'

1.2 What happens first?

Look at the picture on page 1, opposite. What do you think?

1 Who is the baby?
   a A poor child.
   b A child without a family.
   c A prince.

2 What is going to happen to the baby next?
   a Nobody will want him.
   b He is going to live with strangers.
   c He is going to live with his parents.

3 What will happen to him in the future?
   a He will spend his life in the forest.
   b His life will suddenly change.
   c He will run away from his home in the forest.

The Young King

*'This cloth was made by the white hands of pain. There is blood
in the jewels and death in the heart of the pearl.'*

The young king was alone in his beautiful room in the palace. He was only
sixteen years old and he was wild-eyed, like an animal of the forest. The old
king's **servant**s found him in the forest. At that time, the boy believed that he
was the son of a poor forester. He was brought up by the forester. But now he
knew that he was the child of the old king's daughter.

The king's daughter married an ordinary man, a painter. He painted pictures
on the walls of the great church where kings were **crown**ed. But one day he
disappeared, leaving the pictures unfinished. The week-old baby was taken away
from his mother's side while she slept. The forester and his wife had no children,
and the baby was given to them.

The princess died.

servant /ˈsɜːvənt/ (n) someone who works in another person's house
crown /kraʊn/ (v/n) to place a circle of gold on someone's head and make them king or queen

When the old king was dying, he said, 'My heart is heavy because I have done a terrible thing. The crown must not pass away from my family. Bring my daughter's child from the forest. He will be king after me.'

When the boy was brought to the palace, he showed a strange love for beautiful things. He gave a happy cry when he saw his fine new clothes and rich **jewel**s. He quickly took off the old coat that he wore in the forest. He walked through the palace from room to room, looking at everything.

A rich man came to see the young king one day. He found him on his knees in front of a beautiful picture from Venice. On another day, people searched for the king for hours. They finally found him in a little room at the north end of the palace. He was looking at the shape of the Greek **god** Adonis, cut in a jewel.

In bed that night, the young king thought about the beautiful clothes for his special day – a gold coat and a jewelled crown. People were working day and night to finish the clothes in time. The young king imagined himself in the great church, dressed as a king. His eyes closed, and he fell asleep. As he slept, he dreamed.

He dreamed that he was standing in a long, low room. Around him were cloth-makers at work. Only a little daylight came in through narrow windows. The men's faces were pale and thin. Little children were working with them. They were weak and hungry and their little hands shook.

The young king went to watch one of the cloth-makers. The man looked at him angrily.

'Why are you watching me?' he said. 'Did our employer ask you to watch us?'

'Who is your employer?' asked the young king.

'He is a man like me. But unlike me, he wears fine clothes. And while I am hungry, he has too much food.'

'You are not a **slave**,' said the young king. 'Your employer does not own you.'

'The rich make the poor their slaves,' answered the cloth-maker. 'We must work to live. But they pay us too little and we die. Men call us free, but we *are* slaves. But these things do not matter to you. You are not one of us: your face is too happy.'

He turned away and continued his work. Then the young king saw that the cloth-maker was making gold cloth. He felt a sudden fear.

jewel /ˈdʒuːəl/ (n) a small, expensive stone
god /gɒd/ (n) the one who made the world and everything in it, in some religions. In other religions there is more than one *god*.
slave /sleɪv/ (n) someone who is owned by another person. A *slave* must work for his or her owner without pay.

'Who are you making that cloth for?' he asked.

'I am making it for the crowning of the young king.'

The young king woke up with a loud cry. He was in his own room in the palace. Through the window, he saw the golden moon hanging in the sky.

◆

The young king fell asleep again and dreamed. He dreamed that he was on a ship. Hundreds of slaves were working on the ship. They were wearing only simple cloths round their waists, and each man was tied to the man next to him. The hot sun shone down on them without pity. A man ran up and down between the slaves. He hit them until the blood came. 'Work faster!' he ordered.

At last the ship stopped near some land. The seamen took one of the youngest slaves, tied a stone to his feet and let him down over the side of the ship. After some time they pulled him out of the water. He had a **pearl** in his right hand. The seamen took it from him, then pushed him back into the water.

The young slave came up again and again; each time he brought with him a beautiful pearl. The seamen put the pearls in a green bag.

Then the slave came up for the last time. This time he brought the best pearl of all. It was shaped like the full moon and it was brighter than the morning star. But the face of the slave was strangely white. He fell down on the ship, and blood came from his ears and mouth.

'Dead?' cried one of the seamen. 'Throw the body into the sea.' He looked at the pearl. 'This will be for the crowning of the young king.'

When the young king heard this, he woke up with a great cry. Through the window, the stars were growing weak and daylight was coming.

◆

The young king fell asleep again and dreamed. He was walking through a dark forest full of strange fruit and flowers. He continued walking until he came out of the forest. There he saw a great crowd of men, working in a dry river. They were making large holes in the ground and breaking the rocks with tools.

The young king turned and saw an old man standing behind him, with a mirror in his hand.

'Who are these men?' he asked.

'The people in the walled cities have no food, and little water,' said the old man. 'But these men are working in the river to find—'

'What are they trying to find?'

'Jewels – for a king's crown,' said the old man.

'For which king?'

'Look in the mirror and you will see him.'

pearl /pɜːl/ (n) something small, white, round and beautiful that is found in a sea animal

4

The young king looked in the mirror and saw his own face. He woke up with a great cry. Bright sunlight was shining into the room, and in the garden outside birds were singing in the trees.

◆

Government officers came into the young king's room and greeted him. Servants brought the coat made of gold cloth. Other servants placed the crown and fine jewels in front of him.

The young king looked at the lovely things. They were very beautiful. But he remembered his dreams, and said, 'Take them away. I will not wear them.'

The government officers were very surprised. Some of them thought that he was joking. They laughed.

He spoke to them again: 'Take these things away. I will not wear them. This cloth was made by the white hands of pain. There is blood in the jewels and death in the heart of the pearl.' And he told them his three dreams.

When the men heard this, they said to him, 'You do not know what you are saying. A dream is only a dream – it is not real. We cannot worry about the people who work for us. And if you do not wear these clothes and this crown, you will not look like a king. How will the people know that you *are* king?'

'Perhaps you are right,' answered the young king. 'But I will not wear this coat and I will not wear this crown. I did not wear fine clothes when I came into the palace. I will go out of the palace in the same way. Go, all of you. Only this boy may stay.'

The government officers and the servants left. Only one servant, a boy, stayed with the king. The young king opened a big box and took out a rough coat. This was his coat in the days when he watched animals on the hillside for the forester. The young king also took out a stick from the forest.

The boy said, 'Sir, where is your crown?'

The young king cut a piece from a wild rose that grew near the window. He made it into a circle and put it on his head.

'This will be my crown,' he said.

The young king left his room. The government officers were waiting for him. He got up on his horse and rode out through the great gates of the palace towards the church. The boy ran with him.

The people in the streets laughed. 'This is not the king,' they said as he rode past them. He stopped and answered, 'I am the king.' And he told them his three dreams.

A man came out of the crowd and spoke angrily to him: 'The life of the poor comes from the fine things that rich people use. When we make these things, we can buy bread. Go back to your palace and put on your king's clothes. Why are you worrying about us?'

'Aren't rich people and poor people brothers?' asked the young king. His eyes filled with tears as he rode through the angry cries of the people. The boy became afraid and left him.

At the great gate of the church, the soldiers tried to stop him. 'Only the king can come in here,' they said to him.

'I *am* the king,' he answered angrily, and he pushed through them.

The most important **priest** in the church was waiting to crown the new king. He saw the young king in his poor clothes, and he went to meet him.

'My son,' he said. 'Is this how a king dresses? What crown shall I crown you with? This should be a day of great happiness.'

'Can happiness wear what sadness and pain have made?' said the king, and he told the High Priest his dreams.

priest /priːst/ (n) someone who works in a church or other religious place

'I am an old man,' answered the High Priest. 'I know that many wrong things are done in the world. But God has made us this way, and He is wiser than you. The weight of this world's suffering is too heavy for one man.'

'Can you say that in this house of God?!' said the young king. He walked past the High Priest and went down on his knees.

Suddenly a loud noise came from the street outside. The government officers came into the church, shouting, 'Where is this dreamer of dreams? Where is the king who is dressed as a servant? He cannot be our king!'

The young king stood up and turned sadly towards them. Then sunlight shone down through the coloured glass of the church windows. It changed his coat into a coat that was more beautiful than one of gold cloth. From the dead stick, white flowers grew that were more beautiful than pearls. The wild roses on his head shone brighter than jewels.

He stood there dressed as a king. The light of God filled the place and there was music and singing. The people fell on their knees.

The High Priest laid his hands on the young king's head. 'Someone has crowned you who is greater than me,' he said, and he went down on his knees in front of his king.

The Birthday of the Infanta

*He caught the flower and kissed it. Then he put his hand on
his heart and went down on one knee in front of her.*

It was the birthday of the Infanta, the daughter of the King of Spain. She
was twelve years old. The little princess was playing with her friends in the
sun-filled palace garden. From a window in the palace, the king watched her.
The Infanta looked just like her mother. The king thought sadly about his
young French queen. She died soon after her child was born, before she saw the
beautiful flowers in the garden and the fruit on the trees.

His love was great, and he could not hide her body in the ground. So an
Egyptian doctor worked on her body. It stayed as fresh after death as it was in
life. Twelve years later, it still lay in the small palace church. Once every month
the king went there and fell down on his knees by her side. He called out, 'My
queen! My queen!'

Today, the king watched the Infanta playing in the garden. Memories of his married life returned to him. The Infanta had the same pretty ways as the queen. She moved her head in the same way when she talked. She had the same proud, beautiful mouth, the same wonderful smile. But the king felt very sad. He could not enjoy the children laughing or the sunny garden. When the Infanta looked up again at the window, he was not there.

'Why has he gone away,' she said, 'when I want him to stay with me on my birthday? Where is he? Has he gone to that dark little church where I cannot go? He is very silly! The sun is shining so brightly and everyone is so happy!'

She walked to a big tent to watch her birthday show. Don Pedro, her uncle, went with her. The Camarera went too. She was a great lady who looked after the Infanta. At the show, some boys rode on wooden horses, dressed in bright clothes. An Indian man played music on a pipe and made **magic**. He covered the sand with a cloth, and a tree grew up out of it. Then flowers grew on the tree. He brought eggs out of his nose. Then he took one egg and changed it into a little bird. The bird flew away, and the children were excited and happy.

Some schoolboys did a beautiful dance. Then some Africans sat in a ring and played music. Another man brought in a dog. The animal stood up on its back legs and danced.

But the funniest thing was the dancing of an ugly little **dwarf**. He had very short legs and a very big head. The children laughed and laughed at him. The Camarera told the Infanta to be quieter. A princess must not laugh so loudly.

The dwarf was found by two rich Spanish men when he was running wild in the forest. His father happily sold his ugly child to them, and they took him to the palace as a surprise for the Infanta. There was one very funny thing about the dwarf. He did not seem to know how strange and ugly he looked. He seemed quite happy! When the children laughed, he laughed too.

The Infanta was very amused by him. He could not keep his eyes off her; he seemed to dance just for her. At the end of his dance, she took a white rose out of her hair and threw it to him. He caught the flower and kissed it. Then he put his hand on his heart and went down on one knee in front of her. He was smiling, and his little eyes were bright.

The Infanta laughed at this for a long time. She wanted the dwarf to dance again. But the Camarera said, 'The sun is too hot. The Infanta should go back to the palace for her birthday dinner. The dwarf can dance again for you later.' So the Infanta went back to the palace, and the other children followed her.

◆

magic /'mædʒɪk/ (n) strange, special skills; a *magician* can do impossible or unbelievable things
dwarf /dwɔːf/ (n) an imaginary person in stories who looks like a small man

The little dwarf was very, very proud. He ran out into the garden, kissed the white rose and jumped up and down happily. He told the flowers: 'The Infanta has given me this beautiful white rose. She wants me to dance for her a second time.' They moved their heads, but they did not seem to hear him. He told the birds, but they did not stop singing. Perhaps their song was about him and the Infanta.

'The Infanta has given me a white rose and she loves me. Oh, I want to be with her in the palace. I can be her friend and play with her and teach her nice things. I can make a pipe and play music on it for her. I can teach her how to call the birds. Yes! She must come to the forest and play with me. We will dance on the fresh grass. When she is tired, I will find a soft bank of flowers for her. Then she can rest on it.'

He looked at the palace. The doors and windows were shut to keep out the midday heat. Then he saw a little door which was open. He went through it. He was in a beautiful room. There was gold everywhere, and the floor was made of coloured stones. But the little Infanta was not there.

The dwarf came to a second room. In the centre there was a big round table with red books on it. This was the room where the government officers met. The little dwarf was afraid, but he thought of the pretty Infanta. 'I must continue,' he said, 'and find her. I will tell her that I love her. I will ask her to come away with me after my dance. I know that she will come to the forest with me.' He smiled as he thought of it.

He went into the next room. This was the brightest and the most beautiful of all the rooms. The tables and chairs were made of silver, and the floor was of sea-green stone. But he was not alone!

He saw someone – a small person – standing in the shadow at the other end of the room. Watching him! He shouted with excitement, and moved out into the sunlight. As he moved, the other one moved too. He saw it clearly. This was not the Infanta! It was a terrible, ugly thing. It was not shaped like other people. It had short legs and long arms, and its big head was covered with long black hair. He looked angrily at it, and it looked angrily back at him. He laughed, and it laughed. He went towards it, and it came to meet him.

'What is it?' He looked at the rest of the room. He could see everything in this wall of clear water. Every picture, every chair, every table. He took the white rose and kissed it. That other one had a rose too! It kissed it and pressed it to its heart. He was looking at himself in a mirror!

When he realized this, he fell down on the floor. He cried. *He* was the ugly one! The children laughed *at* him, not with him. The little Infanta did not love him; she only laughed at his ugliness.

'Why didn't they leave me in the forest? There were no mirrors there and I never knew. Why didn't my father kill me? Why did he sell me so other people could laugh at me?'

Hot tears poured down his face. He pulled the white rose to pieces and threw the pieces away. The other one did the same. When he looked at it, it looked at him with a face full of pain. He covered his eyes and lay in the shadow.

◆

When the Infanta and her friends came into the room, they saw the ugly little dwarf. He was lying on the floor and hitting it with his hands in the strangest way. They shouted happily and stood round and watched.

'His dancing was very funny,' said the Infanta, 'but this is funnier.'

The little dwarf did not look up. He lay there, crying very quietly. Then he made a strange noise and put his hand on his side. Then he fell back and lay there.

'That was wonderful!' said the Infanta. 'But now you must dance for me.'

'Yes,' cried the children. 'Get up and dance!' But the little dwarf did not answer.

The Infanta was angry and called her uncle. He was walking with the king's doctor in the garden outside.

'My funny little dwarf is not listening to me,' she cried. 'You must wake him up. Tell him to dance for me!'

Don Pedro hit the dwarf. 'You must dance,' he said. 'The Infanta of Spain wants to see you dance.'

But the little dwarf did not move. The king's doctor looked at the dwarf and put his hand on the little man's heart. 'Oh, princess,' he said, 'your funny little dwarf will never dance again. That is very sad, because he is very, very ugly. Even the king laughed at him.'

'Why won't he dance again?' asked the Infanta.

'Because his heart is broken. He did not want to live, and he is dead.'

The Infanta was angry. 'In future,' she cried, 'I will only play with people who have no hearts.' And she ran out into the garden.

2.1 Were you right?

Look back at your answers to Activity 1.2 on page iv. Then decide if these sentences about 'The Young King' are right (✓) or wrong (✗).

1 ☐ The young king was born in the forest.
2 ☐ His father was a king.
3 ☐ His mother was a princess.
4 ☐ His mother didn't want him.
5 ☐ One day he was taken from the forest to the palace.

2.2 What more did you learn?

1 The young king has three dreams. Put these words in the right places.

a slave ship	a long, low room	a dark forest
men breaking rocks	thin, pale faces	dead and bloody men
good cloth	a search for jewels	pearls from the sea

The first dream
....
....
....

The second dream
....
....
....

The third dream
....
....
....

2 Discuss these questions.

a How does the young king dress on the day he is crowned? Why?
b What happens in the church? Why?

2.3 Language in use

Look at the sentences in the box. Then finish these sentences about 'The Birthday of the Infanta'.

> She moved her head in the same way **when** she talked.
>
> **When** the children laughed, he laughed too.

1 The Infanta's mother died soon after ....

2 The king thinks of his dead wife when ....

3 When the children laugh at the dwarf's dancing, ...

....

4 The dwarf believes in the Infanta's love for him after ....

....

5 Until he looks in a mirror, ...

6 Before he dies, ...

7 The Infanta is very angry when ....

2.4 What's next?

Look at this picture from the next story, 'The Happy Prince'. What do you think the bird and the prince are saying? Write their conversation.

Bird: ....

....

Prince: ....

....

....

....

Bird: ....

....

Prince: ....

....

....

....

The Happy Prince

'It is very cold, but I feel quite warm.'
'That is because you have done a good thing,' said the prince.

The **statue** of the Happy Prince stood high above the city. It was covered with gold, its eyes were bright blue jewels, and a red jewel hung from its waist. Everyone thought that it was very beautiful.

'Why aren't you like the Happy Prince?' mothers said to their little boys when they cried.

statue /ˈstætʃuː/ (n) something that looks like a person or animal. *Statues* are usually made of stone or metal.

16

Sad men looked at the statue and said, 'I am glad that someone in the world is happy.'

One night a little bird flew alone over the city. The other birds were all in Egypt now. 'Where can I stay tonight?' he thought. Then he saw the statue. 'I will stay there,' he thought. 'It is high up, so there is plenty of fresh air.'

He landed between the feet of the Happy Prince. 'I have a golden bedroom!' he thought. But as he put his head under his **wing**, a large drop of water fell on him.

He looked up. 'That is very strange!' he thought. 'There is not a cloud in the sky, but it is raining!'

Then another drop fell. 'I cannot stay on a statue that does not keep me dry,' he thought. 'I must find another place.' And he decided to fly away. But as he opened his wings, a third drop fell. He looked up and saw – Ah! What did he see?

The eyes of the Happy Prince were full of tears. Tears ran down his golden face. The face was very beautiful in the moonlight, and the bird felt sorry for him.

'Who are you?' asked the bird.

'I am the Happy Prince.'

'Then why are you crying? I am wet with your tears.'

'When I was alive,' said the prince, 'I had a heart like every other man. But I did not know what tears were. I lived in a palace where there was no sadness. In the daytime I played with my friends in a beautiful garden, and in the evening I danced. There was a high wall round the garden. But I did not know what lay on the other side. So I was called the Happy Prince. I was pleased with my little world. Now I am dead, and they have put me up here. I can see all the unhappiness of my city. My heart now is made of a cheap metal. But even that poor heart can feel, and so I cry.'

'Oh,' said the bird to himself, 'he is not all gold – he is only gold on the outside.'

'Far away from here,' said the Happy Prince in a low voice, 'there is a poor house in a little street. Through an open window, I can see a woman at a table. Her face is very thin and she has rough, red hands. She is making a dress for one of the queen's ladies, for a dance in the palace. Her little boy is lying on a bed in the corner of the room. He is very ill. He is crying because she can only give him water from the river. Little bird, will you take my red jewel to her? I cannot move from here.'

'My friends are waiting for me in Egypt,' said the bird.

'Little bird, little bird,' said the prince, 'please stay with me for one night and do this for me. The boy is crying and his mother is so unhappy.'

wing /wɪŋ/ (n) one of the two parts of a bird's body that help it fly

The Happy Prince looked very sad, and the little bird was sorry for him. 'It is very cold here,' he said, 'but I will stay with you for one night. Tomorrow I will take the jewel.'

'Thank you, little bird,' said the prince.

◆

So the bird took the great red jewel from the prince's waist and flew away with it over the roofs of the town. He passed the palace and heard the sound of dancing.

A beautiful girl was at a window with her lover. 'I hope my dress will be ready for the dance next week,' she said. 'Those women are so lazy.'

The bird passed over the river and flew and flew. At last he came to the poor little house and looked inside. The boy was lying on the bed. The mother was asleep; she was so tired. He flew in and put the great red jewel on the table. Then he flew round the bed, moving the air around the boy's face with his wings.

'Oh,' said the boy, 'my face does not feel so hot. I think I am getting better.' And he fell asleep.

Then the bird flew back to the Happy Prince. 'It is strange,' the bird said. 'It is very cold, but I feel quite warm.'

'That is because you have done a good thing,' said the prince. The little bird fell asleep.

◆

When day came, the bird flew down to the river for a bath. A clever man saw him. 'That is very unusual!' he said. 'That kind of bird, here in winter! I must write that down!'

'I will go to Egypt tonight,' thought the bird.

When the moon came up, he flew back to the Happy Prince. 'Can I do anything for you in Egypt?' he said.

'Little bird, little bird,' said the prince, 'please will you stay with me for one more night?'

'My friends are waiting for me,' answered the bird.

'Far away across the city,' said the prince, 'I can see a young writer in a little room at the top of a house. He is sitting at a table that is covered with papers. At his side there are some dead flowers. He is trying to finish a story. But he is very cold and he cannot write. There is no fire in the room, and he is weak and hungry.'

'I will wait with you for one more night,' said the bird kindly. 'What shall I take to him?'

'Take him one of my eyes,' said the prince. 'They are made of beautiful blue stones from India. The young man can sell it and buy wood and food. He can finish his story.'

'Take out your eye, dear prince?' said the bird. 'I cannot do that!' And he began to cry.

'Do it!' said the prince.

So the bird took out the prince's eye and flew away to the young man's room. It was easy to get in because there was a hole in the roof. The young man was sitting with his head in his hands, so he did not hear the bird's wings. When he looked up, a beautiful blue jewel was lying on the dead flowers.

'Someone likes my stories!' he cried happily. 'This is a gift from someone who has read my books. Now I can finish writing this story!'

◆

On the next day the bird flew down to the river. He watched the seamen working on the ships. 'I am going to Egypt!' he cried, but no one listened to him.

When the moon came up, he flew back to the Happy Prince. 'I have come to say goodbye to you,' he said.

'Little bird, little bird,' said the prince, 'please will you stay with me for one more night?'

'It is winter,' answered the bird. 'The snow will soon come. In Egypt the sun is warm and the trees are green. Dear prince, I must leave you; but I will never forget you.'

'A little girl is standing there in the square below. She is selling eggs. Her eggs have fallen on the ground and they are broken. She has no money to take home. Her father will hit her. Take out my other eye and give it to her.'

'I will stay with you for one more night,' said the bird, 'but I cannot take out your other eye. You will not be able to see!'

'Do it!' said the prince.

So the bird took out the prince's other eye and flew down with it. He flew to the girl and put the jewel in her hand.

'This is a beautiful piece of glass!' cried the little girl. She ran home, laughing.

Then the bird flew back to the prince. 'You cannot see now,' he said, 'so I will stay with you.'

'No,' said the poor prince, 'you must go to Egypt.'

'I will stay with you,' repeated the bird, and he slept at the prince's feet.

The next day he stayed with the prince. He told the prince stories about the strange lands that he knew.

'Dear little bird,' said the prince, 'you are telling me about strange and wonderful things, but the suffering of men and women is stranger than anything. Fly over my city, little bird. Tell me what you see there.'

So the swallow flew over the great city. He saw the rich eating and drinking in their beautiful houses. He saw the poor people sitting at the gate. He flew into the dark streets and saw the white faces of hungry children with sad eyes. Under a bridge, two little boys were lying close together to keep warm. 'We are so hungry!' they said. 'You cannot lie there!' shouted a guard.

Then the bird flew back and told the prince.

'I am covered with fine gold,' said the prince. 'Take it off, piece by piece, and give it to my poor people.'

The bird pulled off the gold, until the Happy Prince looked grey and ugly. The bird took the gold to the poor, and the children's faces became brighter. 'We have bread now!' they cried.

◆

Then the snow came. Ice followed the snow, and hung down from the roofs of the houses. Everyone wore thick coats.

The little bird became colder. He did not leave the prince, because he loved him too much. But he was dying.

'Goodbye, dear prince!' he said. 'Can I kiss you?'

'I am glad that you are going to Egypt,' said the prince. 'You have stayed too long. Kiss me, because I love you.'

'I am not going to Egypt,' said the bird. 'I am going to the House of Death.' He kissed the prince, and fell down dead at his feet. Then there was a strange sound inside the statue. CRACK – the metal heart broke into two pieces.

Early next morning, an important man in the city was walking below with two of his friends. He looked up at the statue. 'The Happy Prince does not look very bright!' he said. 'The red stone has disappeared, his eyes are not there, and he is not golden. He looks like a **beggar**.'

'Yes, he does!' said the man's friends.

'Here is a dead bird at his feet!' said the officer. 'We must make an order that birds cannot die here.'

They pulled down the statue of the Happy Prince and put it in the fire. A stream of bright metal ran out.

beggar /ˈbegə/ (n) someone who asks people for food and money

'This is strange!' said the workmen. 'This broken piece in the middle of the statue has stayed hard. We must throw it away.' So they threw it away with the dead bird.

◆

God said to his servants, 'Bring me the two best things in the city.' They brought Him the broken heart and the dead bird.

'Yes, you have brought the right things,' God said. 'This little bird will sing for ever in my garden, and the Happy Prince will stand in my city of gold.'

3.1 **Were you right?**

Look back at your answers to Activity 2.4. Then circle the right words in these sentences.

1 The bird realises *immediately / soon* that the prince is crying.

2 The bird wants to spend the night in a *wet / dry* place.

3 He feels *angry with / sorry for* the prince.

4 The prince *is / was* very happy.

5 His metal heart *can / can't* feel.

6 From his high place, he can see the *happiness / unhappiness* of people in the city.

3.2 **What more did you learn?**

1 **Match the pictures with the descriptions.**

1 He is given a red jewel.
2 He is seen washing in a river.
3 A dress is being made for her.
4 He is given a beautiful blue stone.
5 She is also given a blue jewel.
6 His gold is given to the poor.

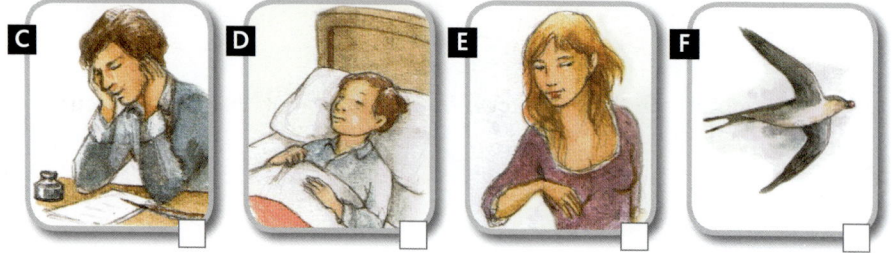

2 **What happens to the prince and the bird at the end of the story? Finish these sentences.**

a The bird becomes very ...., and he .... at the prince's feet. He is taken to ...., to .... in his garden.

b The prince's heart breaks into .... pieces after the death of the .... His statue is .... by workmen, but later stands in God's .... of gold.

3.3 **Language in use**

Look at the sentences on the right. Then look at the picture and finish the questions and answers below. Use present perfect verb forms.

> 'This is a gift from someone who **has read** my books.'
>
> 'The red stone **has disappeared**.'

1 'What ...... *has happened* ...... to the statue of the Happy Prince?' (happen)

   'It .... all its jewels, and its gold covering.' (lose)

2 'Where .... the red jewel from the prince's waist ....?' (go)

   'The bird .... the red jewel to a sick

   boy and his mother.' (take)

3 'Why .... the prince's eyes

   ....?' (disappear)

   'The bird .... the jewels to a

   hungry writer and a frightened child.' (carry)

4 'What .... the prince

   .... with the gold that covered

   him?' (do)

   'He .... it to poor people who

   need the money.' (give)

3.4 **What's next?**

Look at the pictures in the next story. What do you think the story is about? Make notes.

Notes

The Fisherman and his Soul

The young fisherman said, 'I do not need my soul. I cannot see it.
I cannot touch it. Of course I will send it away!'

The young fisherman went out in his boat every evening and threw his **net**s into the water. Sometimes he did not catch much. But sometimes the fish came in from the deep sea and swam into his nets. Then he took them and sold them in the town.

One evening the net was very heavy. The young fisherman laughed. 'Perhaps I have caught all the fish in the sea!' he thought. He pulled and pulled, and the net came nearer and nearer to the boat. At last it came to the top of the water. There were no fish in it – only a sleeping **mermaid**. Her hair was like gold; her body was silver and pearl. She was very beautiful. The young fisherman picked her up in his arms.

net /net/ (n) a piece of material with holes in it that you catch fish with
mermaid /ˈmɜːmeɪd/ (n) an imaginary woman in stories with a fish's tail and no legs

When he touched her, she opened her deep-blue eyes with fear. She tried to escape, but he held her tightly.

She began to cry. 'Please, please don't take me away!' she said. 'I am the daughter of the King of the Sea. He only has me, and he is old and alone.'

The fisherman answered, 'You can go if you make a promise. When I call you, you must come to me. You must come to me and sing. The fish love the song of the People of the Sea. They will come and my nets will be full.'

So the mermaid promised. The fisherman opened his arms, and she disappeared into the water.

◆

Every evening after that, when the young fisherman went out in his boat, he called to the mermaid. She came up out of the water and sang the songs of the People of the Sea. She sang about the king's palace, with its roof of clear blue jewels and its pearl floor. She sang about the gardens of the sea. The big fish came in from the deep sea to listen to her songs. Then the young fisherman threw his nets round them and caught them. When his boat was full, the mermaid disappeared into the sea.

The mermaid never came close to him. Once he tried to touch her, but she went down into the water. He did not see her again that day. Each day the sound of her voice became sweeter in his ears. He forgot about his nets and his boat. The fish came, but he did not see them. He sat in his boat and listened. Darkness closed round him, and the moonlight changed his brown arms to silver.

One evening the young fisherman called to the mermaid, 'Little mermaid, I love you. Take me as your husband.'

But the mermaid answered, 'No, you have a man's **soul**. Send away your soul, and I will love you.'

The young fisherman said, 'I do not need my soul. I cannot see it. I cannot touch it. Of course I will send it away!' He held out his arms. 'I will send my soul away and you will be my wife. We will live in the deepest part of the sea, and you will show me the wonderful things in your songs.'

The little mermaid laughed with happiness and hid her face in her hands.

'But how can I send my soul away?' cried the fisherman. 'Tell me how to do it.'

'I do not know,' said the little mermaid. 'The People of the Sea have no souls.' She looked at him sadly and swam away.

soul /səʊl/ (n) the part of you that, in many religions, continues to exist after your death

◆

Early the next morning the young fisherman went to a priest's house. 'Father,' he said, 'I am in love with one of the People of the Sea. But I cannot marry her because I have a soul. Tell me how to send my soul away. I do not need it. I cannot see it. I cannot touch it.'

The priest answered, 'Stupid man! Your soul was given to you by God. It is the most important thing that you have. It is like the gold and jewels of kings. The People of the Sea have no souls and, like animals, do not know right from wrong.'

'Father,' said the young fisherman, 'I caught the daughter of the King of the Sea in my net. She is more beautiful than the morning star, and whiter than the moon. I will give my soul for her body. I must send my soul away.'

'Go away! Go away!' cried the priest.

The young fisherman went into the city. The market-sellers called to him, 'What are you selling today?'

'I will sell my soul. I do not need it.'

The market-sellers laughed at him. 'We do not want to buy your soul. What can we do with it? Sell us your body and become a slave, but do not talk about your soul.'

The young fisherman thought, 'This is very strange. The priest tells me that a soul costs more than gold and jewels. I do not understand.' He went down by the sea to think.

At last he remembered that there was a **witch** near the beach. He ran along the sand to the place where she lived. She knew by magic that he was coming. She laughed and waited for him.

'What do you want?' she cried, as he ran towards her. 'I can give you anything, but everything has its price.'

'I only want one small thing,' said the young fisherman. 'But the priest was angry when I asked him for it. And the market-sellers laughed at me. So I have come to you.'

'What do you want?' asked the witch, coming nearer.

'I want to send my soul away from me,' answered the young fisherman.

'What will you give me if I help you?' asked the witch, looking at him with her beautiful eyes.

'Five pieces of gold, and my nets, my house and my boat. But tell me how I can lose my soul.'

She laughed. 'I am a witch. I can have all the gold and silver that I want.'

'So what shall I give you? What shall I do?'

witch /wɪtʃ/ (n) a woman who is believed to do strange, bad things

28

She put her thin white hand on his head and smiled at him. 'You must dance with me, pretty boy,' she said.

'Only that? Nothing more?' cried the young fisherman.

'Only that,' she answered, and she smiled at him again.

'We must dance when the moon is full. Tonight you will come to the top of the mountain. It is the witches' meeting place, and He will be there.'

'Who is "He"?' asked the young fisherman.

'Come tonight. Stand near the tree on the top of the mountain and wait for me. When the moon is full, I will be with you. Then we will dance together on the grass.'

'But you will help me to send my soul away?'

The sunlight shone on her red hair. 'I will,' she answered.

'You are the best of witches,' cried the young fisherman, 'and I will dance with you tonight.'

He smiled at her. Then he ran happily back to the town.

The witch watched him as he went. 'He will be mine!' she said. 'I am as beautiful as she is.'

◆

That evening, the young fisherman climbed to the top of the mountain and stood under the tree in the moonlight. The sea lay far down below, and the shadows of the fishing boats moved on the water.

At midnight the witches came flying through the air.

'Phew!' they said, as they came down to the ground. 'What is this smell? There is a stranger here!'

The young witch came last. She wore a gold dress and her long red hair flew out behind her. 'Where is he? Where is he?' cried the witches when they saw her.

She laughed and ran to the tree and took the fisherman's hand. She pulled him out into the moonlight and began to dance with him. The other witches began to dance too, round and round. Then there was the sound of a horse, but he could not see a horse. He felt afraid.

'Faster! Faster!' cried the witch. She put her arms round his neck. He knew that something terrible was watching him. Then he saw someone under the shadow of a rock.

It was a man, dressed in black. His face was white, but his mouth was like a red flower. His hands were white and heavy with rings. He watched the young fisherman as he danced. Suddenly the dancers stopped and went to kiss the man's hands. He smiled proudly, but he was still looking at the fisherman.

'Now we must go to him,' said the witch, and the fisherman followed her. But when he was close to the man, the young fisherman suddenly called out God's name. He did not know why he called it.

The witches cried out and flew away. The man closed his eyes in pain. He called to his horse, jumped up on to its back, then turned and looked sadly at the fisherman.

The witch with the red hair tried to fly away too, but the fisherman caught her arm and held her.

'Take your hand off me!' she cried.

'No!' he answered. 'First, you must tell me the secret.'

'What secret?' said the witch, fighting like a wild cat.

'You know!' he answered.

There were tears in her green eyes. 'I am as beautiful as the Daughter of the Sea,' she said.

He pushed her away. 'If you do not keep your promise, I will kill you.'

Her face was grey. 'All right,' she said. 'It is your soul, not mine.' She took out a little knife in a green case. 'The shadow of the body is the body of the soul. Stand by the sea, with your back to the moon. Cut your shadow away from your feet and order your soul to leave you.'

He took the knife. Then he began to climb down the mountain. His soul inside him called out, 'I have lived with you for many years and I have been your servant. Do not send me away from you! How have I hurt you?'

The young fisherman laughed. 'You have not hurt me, but I do not need you. My love is calling me.' He stood on the sand, with his back to the moon. His shadow lay in front of him.

His soul said, 'If I must go away, do not send me away without a heart. There is no love or kindness in the world, and I am afraid. I need to take your heart with me.'

'My heart belongs to my love,' he answered. 'So do not wait – go! I do not need you.'

The young fisherman took the little knife out of its case and cut away the shadow from round his feet. It stood up in front of him. It was just like him. He stepped back and put away the knife. He was afraid. 'Go!' he said. 'I never want to see you again!'

'No! We *must* meet again,' said the soul.

'How will we meet?' cried the young fisherman. 'Will you follow me into the deepest part of the sea?'

'Once every year I will come to this place and call to you,' said the soul. 'Perhaps you *will* need me.'

'Why will I need you?' cried the young fisherman. 'But do what you like.' Then he jumped into the sea. The little mermaid came up to meet him. She put her arms round his neck and kissed him. Then they went down into the sea.

The soul went away, crying.

◆

After a year, the soul came down to the sea and called to the young fisherman. He came out of the sea and said, 'Why are you calling me?'

The soul answered, 'Come nearer. I want to tell you about the wonderful things that I have seen.' So the fisherman came nearer and listened. 'When I left you,' the soul said to him, 'I travelled to the east. All wise things come from the east. I arrived at a city, walked through its streets and came to the garden of its god. "I want to see your god," I said to one of the priests, and he took me to a house in the garden. There was no god there, only a metal mirror on a stone table.

'I said to the priest, "Where is the god?"

'He said, "There is no god, but this is a special mirror. It shows everything on earth. When you have this mirror, you know everything. Nothing is hidden from you."

'I stole the mirror and I have hidden it close to here. Take me as your soul again, and you will be wiser than all the wise men.'

The young fisherman laughed. 'Love is better than understanding,' he cried. 'And the little mermaid loves me.' He went back into the sea. The soul went away, crying.

◆

After the second year, the soul came down to the sea and called to the young fisherman. The fisherman came up out of the sea and said, 'Why are you calling me?'

'Come nearer,' the soul answered. 'I want to tell you about the wonderful things that I have seen. When I left you, I travelled to the south. All gold and jewels come from the south. After many days I came to Ashtar. The king of that city has a special ring on his finger. If you have that ring, you are richer than all the kings in the world. I went into the king's palace. The soldiers hit me, but they could not hurt me. The king said, "Who are you? Why can't we hurt you? Please leave here tonight. While you are here, I am not king of this city." I answered, "I will go if you give me your ring."'

Then the soul said to the fisherman, 'I have hidden the ring in a place not far from here. Come with me and take it. You will be richer than all the kings in this world.'

The young fisherman laughed. 'Love is better than gold and jewels,' he cried. 'And the little mermaid loves me.' He went back into the sea. The soul went away, crying.

◆

At the end of the third year, the soul came down to the sea and called to the fisherman. When he came, the soul said, 'Come nearer. I want to tell you about the wonderful things that I have seen. On my journeys I came to a city where there is a house near the river. Seamen come to that house and drink wine. As I sat there, an old man came in. He played music, and a girl came and danced. Her face was covered and I could not see it. But her white feet moved like little birds. They were the most beautiful feet that I have ever seen. It was the most wonderful dancing. It is only a few days' journey from this place.'

The young fisherman remembered that the little mermaid had no feet. She could not dance. So he said, 'All right. It is only a short journey, and then I can return to my love.' He climbed out on to the land and held out his arms to his soul. The soul cried with happiness and went into him.

They travelled all that night and came to a city. As they walked along a street of jewellers, the young fisherman saw a fine silver cup. The soul said to him, 'Take that cup and hide it.' So he took the cup and they left the city quickly.

But then the young fisherman threw the cup away. 'Why did you tell me to take that cup?' he said to his soul. 'It was wrong.'

But his soul answered, 'It does not matter.'

On the evening of the second day, they came to another city. As they walked along the street, the young fisherman saw a child with a pot of water. His soul said to him, 'Hit that child.' So he hit the child, and the child cried. Then they left the city quickly.

But then the young fisherman became angry. 'Why did you tell me to hit that child? It was wrong.'

But his soul answered, 'It does not matter.'

Late on the evening of the third day, they came to another city. The young fisherman sat down and rested. After some time, a man came past them. 'Why are you sitting here in the street?' he said.

The young fisherman answered, 'I have nowhere to sleep. I have no friends in this city.'

The man said, 'Aren't we all brothers? Didn't one God make us all? Come with me to my house.'

So the young fisherman slept at the man's house. In the middle of the night, his soul woke him and said, 'Go to the man's room. Kill him and take his gold. We need it.' The young fisherman went to the man's room. There was a knife near his bed, and there were three bags of gold. The young fisherman put out his hand and touched the knife, but the man woke up. 'Are you paying for my kindness with blood?' he said.

The soul said, 'Kill him!' So the young fisherman killed the man and took the bags of gold.

When they were away from the city, the young fisherman said, 'Why did you tell me to kill the man? Why did you tell me to take his gold?'

The soul answered, 'It does not matter.'

'No!' cried the young fisherman. 'It *does* matter. Why have you done this to me?'

His soul answered, 'When you sent me out into the world, you did not give me a heart.'

The young fisherman said, 'You are bad. I forget my love when I am with you.' He threw the bags of gold away. 'I sent you away before, and I will send you away again!'

He turned his back to the moon. Then, with the little knife, he tried to cut away the shadow of the body which is the soul. But the soul said, 'A man can only send his soul away once in his life. You must keep me with you for ever.'

The young fisherman said, 'I will go back to the place where the mermaid sang. I will call her. I will tell her about the bad things that I have done.'

His soul said, 'There are many women who are more beautiful. There are the dancing girls of Samaris. They laugh while they dance. Come with me to that city.'

The young fisherman did not answer. He travelled back to the place where his love sang. He called to the little mermaid, but she did not come. He built a hut in the rocks and he called to the mermaid every morning and every night. But she never came up out of the sea to meet him.

◆

A year passed, and the soul thought, 'I have offered him bad things, but his love has been too great. Now I will offer him good things, and perhaps he will come with me.'

So the soul said, 'I have told you about the happiness of the world. Now I will tell you about the world's pain. I will tell you about people who are hungry, poor and sick. Let's go and help those people.'

But the young fisherman did not answer.

◆

A second year passed, and the soul said, 'Your love is stronger than I am. Let me into your heart and then I can be part of you again.'

'Of course you can come in,' said the young fisherman.

'I cannot find a way into your heart,' said his soul. 'There is no room, because your heart is so full of love.'

'I would like to help you,' said the fisherman.

As he spoke, a great sound of crying came from the sea. One of the People of the Sea was dead. The young fisherman left his hut and ran down to the water.

Black waves hurried in to the land and they brought with them the body of the little mermaid. The fisherman threw himself down next to her and held her in his arms. He kissed the cold red mouth.

More waves came. The sound of crying came from the palace of the Sea King. 'The sea is coming,' said his soul. 'If you stay here, it will kill you. Come away.'

But the young fisherman did not listen. 'Love is better than being wise or rich,' he said to the little mermaid. 'Love is beautiful. I was bad and I left you. Then I called you and you did not come. But my love stayed with me and was always strong. Now you are dead, and I will die with you.'

The sea came nearer and tried to cover him with its waves. The fisherman knew that the end was near. He kissed the cold face of the mermaid, and then his heart broke. His soul found a way into it, and became part of him again.

And the sea covered the young fisherman.

4.1 Were you right?

Look back at your answers to Activity 3.4. Then put the sentences below in the right order, 1–12.

a ☐ He cuts out his soul.

b ☐ He asks a priest for help.

c ☐ He does terrible things.

d ☐ He joins the mermaid, under the sea.

e ☐ She promises to sing when he calls to her.

f ☐ He tries to sell his soul.

g ☐ The fisherman's heart breaks.

h ☐ The fisherman accepts an offer from his soul.

i ☐ The mermaid doesn't answer his calls.

j ☐ 1 A fisherman catches a mermaid in his net.

k ☐ He asks her to marry him, but she refuses.

l ☐ He makes an agreement with a witch.

4.2 What more did you learn?

1   Which of these (✓) does the soul offer the fisherman?

2   Which does he accept, and why?

....

4.3 **Language in use**

Look at the sentence on the right. Then complete the sentences below with the right form of each word.

> The young **fisherman** went out in his boat every evening.

1 .... closed around the fisherman. (dark)

2 The little mermaid laughed with .... (happy)

3 'There is a .... here!' (strange)

4 'There is no love or .... in the world.' (kind)

5 'Love is better than ....' (understand)

6 A great sound of .... came from the sea. (cry)

4.4 **What's next?**

1 **Look at this picture. What do you think?**

    a What is the name of the bird in your language?

    ....

    b What is it looking at?

    ....

    c Why?

    ....

    ....

2 **Read the title of the next story, the lines below it, and the first five lines of the story. Which of these do you think <u>don't</u> (✗) happen in the story?**

    a ☐ A student falls in love with a beautiful girl.

    b ☐ The girl isn't interested in him.

    c ☐ The nightingale decides to help the student.

    d ☐ The nightingale searches for a red rose.

    e ☐ She finds one easily.

    f ☐ The student is grateful to the nightingale.

    g ☐ The girl falls in love with the student.

The Nightingale and the Rose

'Death is a great price to pay for a red rose,' cried the nightingale.
'I enjoy life ... But love is better than life.'

'She said, "I will dance with you if you bring me a red rose",' cried the young student, 'but there are no red roses in my garden. I have studied everything that wise men have written. But my life is unhappy because I have no red rose!' His eyes filled with tears.

A little **nightingale** heard him from her old tree.

'Here, at last, is a true lover,' said the nightingale. 'I have sung about true love night after night, but I have never seen a true lover!'

'There will be a dance at the palace tomorrow,' said the student. 'The prince will be there, and my love will be there too. If I bring her a red rose, she will dance with me. If I bring her a red rose, I will hold her in my arms. But there are no red roses in my garden, so I will sit alone. She will not need me, and my heart will break.'

'Yes, he is a true lover, like the lovers in my songs,' said the nightingale. 'Love is happiness to me, but it is pain to him. Love is a wonderful thing. Gold and jewels can never buy it.'

The student cried, 'The musicians will play and my love will dance to the music. Rich men in their fine clothes will crowd round her. But she will not dance with me because I cannot give her a red rose.' He lay down on the grass, put his face in his hands and cried.

'Why is he crying?' asked the little animals in the garden. 'Why is he crying?' asked the flowers.

'He is crying for a red rose,' said the nightingale.

'For a red rose!' they cried, and they laughed. But the nightingale understood. She opened her brown wings and flew up into the air. She passed across the garden like a shadow.

◆

There was a beautiful rose tree standing in the centre of another garden. When she saw it, she flew down to it.

'Give me a red rose,' she cried, 'and I will sing you my sweetest song.'

'I am sorry,' said the rose tree. 'My roses are white – as white as snow. Go to my brother on the other side of the garden. Perhaps he will give you what you want.'

---

nightingale /ˈnaɪtɪŋgeɪl/ (n) a small, wild bird that sings beautifully, usually at night

So the nightingale flew to the other rose tree. 'Give me a red rose,' she cried, 'and I will sing you my sweetest song.'

'I am sorry,' answered the rose tree. 'My roses are yellow – golden yellow. But go to my brother who grows below the student's window. Perhaps he will give you what you want.'

So the nightingale flew to the rose tree which was growing below the student's window.

'Give me a red rose,' she cried, 'and I will sing you my sweetest song.'

'My roses are red,' it answered, 'but the winter cold has frozen my flowers and they have fallen. I will have no roses this year.'

'I only want one red rose,' cried the nightingale, 'only one red rose! How can I get it?'

'There is a way,' answered the tree. 'But I do not want to tell you about it.'

'Tell me the way, please,' said the nightingale. 'I am not afraid.'

'If you want a red rose,' said the tree, 'you must build it out of music by moonlight. The redness must come from your heart's blood. You must sing to

me all night with your heart pressed against a **thorn**. The thorn must cut open your heart and your life blood must run into me and become mine.'

'Death is a great price to pay for a red rose,' cried the nightingale. 'I enjoy life. I love sitting in the green trees and watching the golden sun go down. I love smelling the flowers. But love is better than life, and the heart of a man is more important than the heart of a bird.'

So she opened her brown wings and flew up into the air. She passed over the garden where the young student was still lying in the grass. The tears were not yet dry in his eyes.

'Be happy,' cried the nightingale. 'You will have your red rose. I will build it out of music by moonlight, and I will give my heart's blood for its redness. But you must be a true lover, because love is the wisest and strongest thing.'

The student looked up from the grass and listened. But he could not understand what the nightingale was saying. He only knew things that are written in books. But the old tree loved the little nightingale, and he understood.

'Sing me one last song,' he said. 'I shall be sad and alone when you go.'

thorn /θɔːn/ (n) a sharp, pointed part on a plant - on a rose, for example

So the nightingale sang to the old tree. Her voice was like drops of water falling from a silver cup.

When she finished her song, the student took out a notebook.

'Her voice is beautiful, but her song does not mean anything. It is not really useful because she has no true feelings. She thinks only of her music, not about other people.'

He went into his room, lay down on his bed and thought about his love. After a time, he fell asleep.

◆

When the moon shone in the sky, the nightingale flew to the rose tree. She pressed herself against a thorn. She sang all night, and the cold moon listened. All through the long night she sang, and the thorn went deeper and deeper, and the life-blood ran out of her.

First she sang about the birth of love in the heart of a boy and a girl – and a wonderful rose grew on the highest part of the rose tree. As song followed song, the rose opened. At first it was white – as white as a cloud on a river, as silver as the wings of the early morning.

The rose tree cried to the nightingale, 'Press closer against the thorn, little nightingale. The rose must be red before daylight.'

So the nightingale pressed closer, and her song became louder. Now she sang about the birth of love in the hearts of a man and a woman. The rose became red. But the heart of the rose stayed white, because only the heart's blood of a nightingale can colour the heart of a rose.

The rose tree cried to the nightingale, 'Press closer against the thorn, little nightingale. Or the day will come before the rose is red.'

So the nightingale pressed closer against the thorn. The thorn touched her heart, and pain shot through her. As the pain became worse, her song became wilder. Now she sang of the love which is made perfect by death.

The rose became deep red. The heart of the rose was as red as a jewel. But the nightingale's voice became weaker and weaker. Her little wings stopped moving; her eyes lost their brightness.

She sang a last, wonderful song. The moon heard it and waited in the sky. The red rose heard it and opened wide to the cold morning air.

'Look! Look!' cried the rose tree. 'The rose is ready now.' But the nightingale did not answer, because she was lying dead in the long grass with the thorn in her heart.

◆

At midday, the student opened his window and looked out. 'Ha!' he cried. 'Here is a red rose! It is exactly what I wanted! I have never seen a rose as

beautiful as this. It probably has a long Latin name.' He put out his hand and took it.

Then he put on his hat and ran to the doctor's house with the rose in his hand. The doctor was the student's teacher, and the student loved the doctor's daughter. She was sitting at the door, and her little dog was lying at her feet.

'You wanted me to bring you a red rose,' cried the student. 'Here is the reddest rose in the world. You can wear it tonight, next to your heart. Then we can dance together. And you will know how I love you.'

'I am sorry,' said the girl. 'It will not go with the colour of my dress. And the officer has sent me some real jewels. Everyone knows that jewels cost more than flowers.'

'Thank you very much!' said the student angrily. 'You are very kind!' He threw the rose into the street.

'You cannot speak to me like that,' said the girl. 'Who are you? Only a student!' She got up from her chair and went into the house.

'Love is a very silly thing!' said the student, as he walked away. 'It tells us things which are not going to happen. We believe things which are not true. It is useless. In these difficult times, we must learn useful things. I shall go back to my studies.'

So he returned to his room, took out a big old book, and began to read.

5.1 Were you right?

Look back at your answers to Activity 4.4.2. Then complete the sentences with words from the box.

blood	shape	jewels	happiness	dance	song
old	kindness	cold	theatre	love	colour	gold

1 The student is going to go to a ....

2 The nightingale thinks that love is better than .... or jewels.

3 The roses in the garden are the wrong ....

4 The flowers on the tree under the window were too ...., and have fallen.

5 The nightingale can make a red rose with her ....

6 The girl says that she prefers .... to a rose.

7 The student stops believing in ....

5.2 What more did you learn?

1 Which of these is speaking? Write the numbers, 1–3.

a ☐ 'Here, at last, is a true lover.'

b ☐ 'Love is the wisest and strongest thing.'

c ☐ 'I shall be sad and alone when you go.'

d ☐ 'The day will come before the rose is red.'

e ☐ 'She has no true feelings.'

f ☐ 'Press closer against the thorn.'

g ☐ 'Love is a very silly thing.'

2 Discuss these questions.

a Many people give red roses to people they love. What other presents are usual in your country?

b Who, in the end, do you think has acted well in this story – the nightingale, the girl and/or the student? Why?

5.3 **Language in use**

Look at the sentences on the right.
Then make sentences from the
words below.

> 'I will dance with you if you bring
> me a red rose.'
>
> 'If I bring her a red rose, she will
> dance with me.'

1 if / happy / a red rose / he will be / the student has

   If ....

   ....

2 if / to the girl / he'll sit alone / to the girl / at the dance / he doesn't take one

   If ....

   ....

3 if / with other men / he doesn't dance / she will dance / with her

   If ....

   ....

4 if / the nightingale sings / a rose will grow / all night

   ....

   if ....

5 if / her life blood will run out / against a thorn / she presses her heart

   If ....

   ....

6 if / red / it is covered / the rose will turn / with her blood

   ....

   if ....

5.4 **What's next?**

Talk about the pictures on pages 48 and 57. What do you think happens in the
next story between the two pictures? Write two or three sentences.

....

....

....

....

....

....

The Star Child

The woman said, 'I am your mother.'
He said, 'I am not your son. You are dirty and ugly. Go away!'

Two woodcutters were going home through the forest. It was winter, and very cold. There was thick snow on the ground and on the trees. The river was frozen. The snow was very deep, and the woodcutters went slowly. They were careful, because it is easy to lose your way in the snow.

At last they saw the lights of their village far down below them. They laughed because they were glad. But then they were sad. 'Why do we want to live? Life is so hard for poor people like us.'

Then a strange thing happened: a very bright and beautiful star fell out of the sky. It seemed to fall behind some trees quite near them.

They ran towards it. 'Perhaps there will be a pot of gold where it fell!' they thought.

The first woodcutter reached the place. He saw a coat of gold lying on the white snow. It had silver stars on it. The woodcutters opened the coat to take the pieces of gold from it. But there was no gold. There was only a little child.

One of the men said, 'This is a sad ending to our hopes! We do not need a child. We are poor men and we already have children. We cannot give their food to another child. Let's leave it here.'

The other man said, 'We cannot leave the child here. It will die in the cold. I am as poor as you are. I have many mouths to feed and not much food for them. But I will take the child home with me. My wife will look after it.'

So he picked up the child. He put the coat round it to keep out the cold. Then he went down the hill to his village.

When they came to the village, his friend said, 'You have the child – give me the coat.' But the other man answered, 'That coat isn't ours. It belongs to the child.'

Then he went to his house. His wife opened the door and kissed him.

He said, 'I have found something in the forest and I have brought it to you. I know that you will look after it.'

'What is it?' she asked. 'We need many things.'

He opened the coat and showed her the sleeping child.

'Oh!' she said. 'We have enough children! Why have you brought this strange child to live here?'

'It is a star child,' he said, and he told her about it.

'Our children haven't enough bread. Must we feed another person's child?'

A cold wind from the forest came through the open door. 'Shut the door!' she said. 'The wind is cold.'

He said, 'A cold wind always comes into a house where the heart is cold.'

She did not answer, but went nearer to the fire.

Soon she turned round and looked at him, and her eyes were full of tears. He put the child in her arms. She kissed it and put it in a little bed with her youngest child.

The next day, the woodcutter took the golden coat and put it away in a big box.

◆

The star child grew up with the woodcutter's children. He sat at the table for meals with them and played with them. Every year he became more and more beautiful.

But the star child was only beautiful on the outside. He was proud and unkind. He thought that he was better than the village children. 'They are ordinary people,' he thought, 'but I am the child of a star. They are my servants.'

He threw stones at the poor and at people who asked for help: 'Go to another place and ask for bread! We have none to give you!' He laughed at people who were weak and ugly. He loved himself. In summer, he sat by the water and smiled down at his beautiful face.

The woodcutter and his wife often spoke to him angrily: 'We looked after you when you needed our help. Why are you so unkind to people who need your help?'

The star child did not listen to them. He went back to the other children. He could run fast, and dance, and make music. The other children followed the star child. When he pushed a stick into the eyes of a little **rabbit**, they laughed. When he threw stones at a sick man, they laughed. Their hearts became as hard as his.

◆

One day, a poor woman came through the village. She looked like a beggar. Her clothes were old and dirty, and there was blood on her feet. She sat down under a tree to rest.

The star child saw her and said, 'Look at that ugly old beggar woman. Let's send her away!'

So he came near and threw stones at her. She looked at him with fear in her eyes. The woodcutter saw what the star child was doing. He ran to him and said, 'Why is your heart so cold? What has this poor woman done to you?'

The star child was angry. 'You cannot question me. I am not your son.'

'That is true,' said the woodcutter, 'but I helped you. I was sorry for you when I found you in the forest.'

When the old woman heard this, she made a loud noise. Then she fell to the ground. The woodcutter carried her into the house to his wife. They brought food to her, but she did not eat or drink.

She asked, 'Did you say that the child was found in the forest? Was that ten years ago – ten years ago today?'

'Yes,' said the woodcutter. 'I found him in the forest exactly ten years ago.'

'Did he have a coat of gold with silver stars on it?'

'Yes,' said the woodcutter. He took the coat out of the box and showed it to her.

'He is my little son. I lost him in the forest. I have travelled the world, trying to find him.'

The woodcutter went out and called to the star child: 'Come into the house. Your mother is waiting there for you.'

The star child ran into the house. But when he saw the old woman, he laughed. 'Where is my mother?' he asked. 'I can only see this dirty old beggar woman.'

rabbit /ˈræbɪt/ (n) a small animal with long ears that lives under the ground

The woman said, 'I am your mother.'

He said, 'I am not your son! You are dirty and ugly. Go away! I do not want to see your face again!'

'But it is true. You are my son,' she cried. She fell on her knees and held out her arms to him. 'Thieves stole you from me and left you in the forest. But I knew you when I saw you. And I knew the coat of gold with silver stars. So please come with me. For many years I have tried to find you. Come with me, my son. I need your love.'

But the star child did not move.

At last he spoke, and his voice was hard and angry. 'If you are really my mother, I do not want to know you. I thought that I was the child of a star, not the child of a beggar. So go away. I do not want to see you again!'

'Won't you kiss me before I go?' she cried. 'I suffered so much while I was looking for you.'

'No,' said the star child. 'I will not.'

So the woman went away, crying, into the forest.

The star child was glad and ran back to his friends. But when they saw him, they said, 'Go away, ugly face! You cannot play with us.'

'Why did they say that to me?' thought the star child. He went to the water and looked into it. His face was ugly now. He fell on the grass and cried. 'This has happened to me because I have done wrong,' he thought. 'I have been unkind to my mother and sent her away. I will go and look for her. I will not rest until I find her.'

So he ran away into the forest. He called for his mother all day, but there was no answer. When the sun went down, he slept on the grass. The animals and birds remembered his sticks and stones, and they ran away from him.

In the morning, he walked through the forest. He asked everything he met, 'Have you seen my mother?' But the animals said. 'You pushed sticks into our eyes. You threw stones at us.' And the birds said, 'You cut our wings. You stole our eggs.' The star child cried and asked them to forgive him. Then he continued walking.

On the third day, he came out of the forest and into open country. He passed through villages, and the children threw stones at him. The men sent him away.

◆

The star child searched for three years. Sometimes he seemed to see his mother on the road in front of him. He called to her and ran after her, but he never reached her. People told him, 'No, we have not seen her. Nobody has walked along this road.' They laughed at him.

One evening, he came to the gates of a great city. The soldier at the gate stopped him. 'What do you want here?'

'I am looking for my mother,' he answered. 'I want to come into this city, please. Perhaps she is here.'

'Your mother will not be pleased when she sees you. You are uglier than the ugliest animal. Go away!'

Another soldier said, 'Who is your mother and why are you trying to find her?'

He answered, 'My mother is a beggar. I have been very unkind to her. I want her to forgive me.' But they stopped him going in.

He turned away, crying. Then an officer came. 'Who is trying to come into this city?' he asked.

'A beggar,' they answered, 'and he is the child of a beggar. So we are sending him away.'

'No!' said the officer, laughing. 'We will sell him as a slave. The price will be the price of a loaf of bread.'

A strange old man said, 'I will buy him at that price.' He paid the money and took the star child into the city.

They went along many streets and came to a little door. The old man touched the door with his ring and it opened. They went down five steps into a garden. Then the old man put a cloth over the star child's eyes and pushed him into a building. When the cloth was taken away, the child was in a dark prison.

The old man gave him a piece of bread and said, 'Eat!' And he gave him a cup of water and said, 'Drink!' Then the old man went out. He shut and locked the door.

The old man was really a clever magician.

The next day, he came to the star child and said, 'There is a forest near the south gate of the city. In it there are three pieces of gold. One is white gold, one is yellow gold, and the third is red gold. Today you must bring me the piece of white gold. If you do not bring it back, I will hit you. Go! This evening I will wait for you at the door of the garden.' He put a cloth over the eyes of the star child and took him through the house and the garden and up the five steps to the door. Then he sent him into the street.

The star child went out of the gate of the city and came to the forest. It was a beautiful forest, but the plants under the trees cut his skin. He could not find the piece of white gold anywhere. He looked for it all day. In the evening he turned back, crying.

As the star child came to the end of the wood, he heard a cry. He saw a rabbit. 'Help me! Free me!' it cried.

'I am a slave,' said the star child, 'but I can free you.' So he freed the rabbit.

The rabbit answered, 'You have helped me. What shall I do for you?'

'I am looking for a piece of white gold. I cannot find it.'

'Come with me,' said the rabbit, 'and I will take you to it. I know where it is hidden.'

So the star child went with the rabbit and found the piece of white gold in a tree. The rabbit ran away and the star child went towards the city.

At the gate of the city, there was a man. His face and skin were eaten away by a terrible illness. A grey cloth covered his face and there were two holes in the cloth for his eyes. When he saw the star child, he cried out, 'I have no food. Give me some money or I will die.'

'I only have one piece of gold,' said the star child. 'If I do not take it to my employer, he will hit me.'

The sick man said again sadly, 'Please give me some money, or I shall die.' The star child felt sorry for him and gave him the piece of white gold.

When the star child came to the magician's house, the magician asked, 'Have you got the piece of white gold?'

'No,' said the star child, 'I have not.'

So the magician hit him. Then he said, 'Eat!' but he did not give him any bread. He said, 'Drink', but he gave him a cup with no water in it.

The next day, the magician came to the child and said, 'Bring me the piece of yellow gold today. If you do not bring it, I will hit you harder than yesterday. And I will keep you as my slave.'

The star child went to the forest. All day he tried to find the piece of yellow gold. In the evening, he sat down and began to cry. The little rabbit came to him.

'Why are you crying?' asked the rabbit.

'I am looking for a piece of yellow gold which is hidden here. If I do not find it, my employer will hit me again.'

'Follow me,' said the rabbit, and it ran through the forest to a little stream. The piece of yellow gold was lying in the sand at the bottom of the stream.

'How can I thank you?' said the star child. 'This is the second time that you have helped me.'

'You helped me first,' said the rabbit, and it ran away.

The star child took the piece of yellow gold and hurried back to the city. The sick beggar saw him. He cried out, 'Give me some money, or I will die!'

The star child said, 'I only have one piece of gold. If I do not take it to my employer, he will hit me. He will keep me as his slave.' The sick man cried, and the star child felt sorry for him. He gave him the piece of yellow gold.

When the star child came to the magician's house, the magician opened the door.

'Have you got the piece of yellow gold?'

'No,' said the star child, 'I have not.'

So the magician hit him and put him in the prison.

The next day, the magician came to him and said, 'If you bring me the piece of red gold today, you will be free. But, if you do not bring it, I will kill you.'

The star child went to the forest. He looked for the piece of red gold all day. In the evening, he sat down and cried. The little rabbit came to him.

The rabbit said, 'The piece of red gold is in that hole in the rock behind you.'

'How can I thank you?' said the star child. 'This is the third time that you have helped me.'

'You helped me first,' said the rabbit, and it ran quickly away.

The star child looked in the hole and found the piece of red gold. He hurried back to the city. The sick man saw him coming. He stood in the middle of the road and cried out to him, 'Give me the piece of red gold or I must die.'

The star child gave him the piece of red gold, saying, 'You need it more than I do.' But he was very sad.

As the star child walked through the gate of the city, the soldiers greeted him. 'That is a beautiful young man!' they said. A crowd of people followed him, shouting, 'Nobody in the world is as beautiful as this man!' The star child thought, 'They are laughing at me because I am so unhappy.'

He lost his way in the crowd and suddenly he was in the great square. In that square was the king's palace.

The palace gate opened. Government officers ran out to greet him. They said, 'We have waited for you. You are the son of our king.'

The star child answered, 'I am not a king's son. I am the ugly child of a poor beggar woman.'

Then an officer held up a mirror and asked, 'Why do you think you are not beautiful?'

The star child saw that his face was beautiful again. But something new shone from his eyes. It was love and kindness.

The officers stood in front of him and said, 'Wise men told us about this day a long time ago. We are waiting for you – for our new king. Take this crown and be our king.'

The star child said, 'I cannot be your king, because I have been unkind to my mother. I must find her and ask her to forgive me. I cannot stay here.'

He turned away towards the city gate. Then, in the crowd, he saw the beggar woman who was his mother. At her side stood the sick man.

He cried out in happiness. He ran to them and threw himself down and kissed his mother's feet. 'Mother,' he said, 'I was proud and unkind. Now please forgive me and take me as your son.'

He held out his hands and touched the sick man's feet and said, 'I gave you money three times because I was sorry for you. Ask my mother to speak to me.'

The star child's mother put her hand on his head and said, 'Stand up'.

He stood up and looked at them. Now they were a king and queen.

The queen said, 'This is your father. You helped him when he was the sick man.'

And the king said, 'This is your mother.'

Then they kissed him and took him into the palace.

So the star child became king. He gave bread and clothes to the poor, and was kind and good to everyone.

There was happiness in the land.

6.1 Were you right?

Look back at your answers to Activity 5.4. Then write short answers to these questions.

1 When the woodcutters find the child, what is on its gold coat? ....

2 Who took him from his real mother? ....

3 Why does the star child run away into the forest? ....

4 Where does he go three years later? ....

5 Who puts him in a prison? ....

6 What colour are the gold pieces that he has to look for? ....

7 Which animal helps him find them? ....

8 Why does he become beautiful again? ....

9 Who is 'the sick man'? ....

10 Who is the star child? ....

6.2 What more did you learn?

1 Which of these (✓) does the star child do when he lives in the forest?

2 How does he look when he leaves the forest?

6.3 **Language in use**

Look at the sentences on the right. Then choose the correct verb forms for the sentences below.

> 'For many years I have tried **to find** you.'
>
> He continued **walking**.

1 The soldiers stopped him *to go / going* into the city.

2 The magician told him *to eat / eating*.

3 The star child gave up *to look / looking* for the gold.

4 The rabbit promised *to help / helping* him.

5 The sick man saw him *to come / coming* back from the forest.

6 When the star child arrived at the palace, government officers ran out *to meet / meeting* him.

7 He asked his mother *to forgive / forgiving* him.

6.4 **What's next?**

1 Discuss examples of the actions of a selfish person. How can a person be taught to be less selfish, do you think?

2 Read the title of the next story, and the lines in *italics* below it. How do you think the giant learns not to be selfish?

a ☐ Everyone refuses to talk to him.

b ☐ Nobody helps him when he needs help.

c ☐ Flowers don't grow in his garden.

d ☐ He becomes small and weak.

e ☐ His garden is taken away from him.

f ☐ He is a very lonely man when he dies.

The Selfish Giant

'My garden is my garden,' said the selfish giant.
'No one can play in it. Only me.' So he built a high wall round it.

When the **giant** went away for seven years, the children played in his garden every afternoon on their way back from school.

It was a large and lovely garden. Beautiful flowers grew in the grass, and there were twelve fruit trees. In the spring, the fruit trees were covered with red and white flowers, and later in the year wonderful fruit grew on them. The birds sang

giant /'dʒaɪənt/ (n) a very tall, strong man in stories

60

sweetly in the trees. Sometimes the children stopped their games and listened to them. 'We are so happy here!' they said.

Then, one day, the giant came back. He saw the children playing in his garden. 'What are you doing here?' he shouted in a very loud voice. The children ran away.

'My garden is *my* garden,' said the giant. 'No one can play in it. Only me.' So he built a high wall round it and put up a notice: KEEP OUT. He was a very selfish giant.

♦

So the children had nowhere to play. They tried to play on the road, but the road was dirty and full of hard stones, and they did not like it. After their lessons, they walked round the giant's high wall and talked about the beautiful garden inside. 'We were so happy there!' they said.

The spring came, and there were flowers and little birds all over the country. But in the garden of the selfish giant, it was still winter. The birds did not sing in it because there were no children. The trees forgot to grow flowers. Snow covered the grass, and ice covered the trees with silver. The north wind came, and the rain.

'I cannot understand why the spring is so late,' said the selfish giant. He was sitting at the window of his house and looking out at his cold, white garden. 'I hope there will be a change in the weather.'

But the spring never came, and the summer did not come. When there was golden fruit in every other garden, there was no fruit in the giant's garden. It was always winter there, with the north wind, and snow, and ice and rain.

♦

The giant was lying in bed one morning when he heard some beautiful music. A little bird was singing outside his window. It was the first birdsong in the garden for a very long time, and it seemed to him the most beautiful music in the world. Then the north wind and the rain stopped.

'I believe that spring has come at last!' said the giant. He jumped out of bed and looked out.

His garden was full of children! They were coming in through a hole in the wall and were climbing up into the trees. The giant saw a little child in every tree. The trees were glad to have the children back. They were covered with flowers again. The birds were flying around and singing with happiness, and flowers were looking up through the green grass.

A very small boy was standing in the far corner of the garden. He could not reach up to climb his tree. He was walking round it and crying. That tree was still covered with ice and snow.

'I have been very selfish!' said the giant. 'Now I know why the spring did not come here. I will put the little boy into the tree. Then I will pull down the wall and my garden will be a children's playground for ever.'

He was really sorry about his unkindness. So he went down, opened the door very quietly, and went out into the garden. But when the children saw him, they were afraid.

All the children ran away except the little boy. His eyes were full of tears and he did not see the giant. The giant came quietly behind him. He took the little boy carefully in his hand and put him up into the tree. Then the tree was suddenly covered with flowers, and the birds came and sang in it. The little boy put his arms round the giant's neck and kissed him.

The other children saw that the giant was not bad and selfish now. They came running back.

'It is your garden now, little children,' said the giant, and he pulled down the wall.

When people walked along the road to the town, they could see into the garden. They saw the giant playing with the children. 'That is a beautiful garden!' they said.

The children played all day. In the evening they came to the giant to say goodbye to him.

'But where is your little friend?' he said. 'Where is the little boy that I put into the tree?' The giant loved him best because the little boy kissed him.

'We do not know,' answered the children. 'He has gone away.'

'You must tell him to come tomorrow – he must come tomorrow.' But the children said, 'We do not know where he lives. We only met him today.' The giant felt very sad.

Every afternoon after school, the children came and played with the giant. But the giant's favourite little boy did not come back again. The giant was very kind to the other children. But he wanted to see his first little friend. 'I would really like to see him!' he thought.

◆

Years passed, and the giant became very old and weak. He could not play in the garden now. So he sat in a big chair and watched the children's games and looked at his garden. 'I have many beautiful flowers,' he said, 'but the most beautiful flowers are the children.'

One morning, when he was dressing himself, he looked out of the window. It was winter, but he did not hate the winter now. The spring was only sleeping, and the flowers were only resting. He waited happily for them to come again.

Suddenly he opened his eyes wide. He looked and looked again. Something wonderful was happening! In the far corner of the garden, a tree was covered with beautiful white flowers. The tree was golden, and silver fruit hung down from it. And the little boy was standing under the tree.

The giant ran out into the garden and he hurried across the grass to the child. Then his face became red and angry. 'Who has hurt you?' he said. There was blood on the child's hands, and on his little feet. 'Who has hurt you?' cried the giant. 'Tell me and I will kill him!'

'No,' said the child. 'This pain is the pain of love.'

'Who are you?' asked the giant. He was afraid, and went down on his knees in front of the little child.

'You helped me to play in your garden,' said the child. 'Today you will come with me to my garden in the sky.'

◆

That afternoon the children came into the garden. They found the giant lying dead under the tree. He was covered with white flowers.

1 Work in a small group. Each person should imagine that they are one of these people or birds from the stories (dead or alive!). Tell the group your story and explain your actions. Answer questions from other students.

2 Each of the seven stories teaches us something about life. Work with another student. Choose one story and discuss the lesson in it. Then write down, below, what we learn from it. Do not write the names of the people in it.

The story teaches us that ....

....

....

Give your sentence to another pair of students. Do they know which story you wrote about?

3 With the same other student, discuss these questions.

a   Which story did you enjoy most? Why?
b   Which story would make the best film for children? Why?
c   Which story would make the best film for adults? Why?
d   Which story can people today learn most from? Why?

Imagine that a magazine is asking people for new stories like the ones in this book. The magazine is going to choose the best story. Write a short story, using one or two words from each of these boxes. Then read other students' stories. Which is the best?

| People: | prince | dwarf | giant | bird | witch |
| | woodcutter | beggar | mermaid | | |

| Things: | gold | jewels | coat | rose | crown | mirror | ring |

| Places: | palace | garden | sea | forest | church | city |

....
....
....
....
....
....
....
....
....
....
....
....
....
....
....
....
....
....
....
....
....

The stories in this book teach us the importance of kindness. How can we help other people? Work in small groups.

1 **Discuss these ideas for helping people. Do you think they are good ones, or not? Why?**

a Some famous people take babies from poor countries into their families.

b Some people give money every month to groups ('charities') that help sick and poor people.

c Some people give money when they read about an urgent need in another country.

d Some people ('volunteers') work for no money to help other people.

e Some towns and cities give food and beds to people who live on the streets.

f Some people give money to poor people who ask for it on the streets.

g Some famous singers play music to get money for poor countries.

h Some richer countries give money to poorer countries.

i Some governments give money to people who can't find a job.

j Some famous people talk about problems because reporters listen to them.

2 **Look at this logo. Do you know this charity? How does it try to help people? Look on the Internet if you don't know.**

3 **Find the logo of a national or international charity that has offices in your country. Draw the logo below. Ask other students about the charity's name and work. Then write the correct information.**

Name: ....

Work: ....

....

rabbit

Sight Words

big
is
little
this

This  is big.

dog

4

This  is little.

dog

This  is big.

rabbit

This  is little.

rabbit

This  is big.

cat

This  is little.

cat

This  is big.

bird

This  is little.

bird

This  is big.

horse